Great Meat Recip

Using traditional British Rare Breeds

Compiled by

The Rare Breeds Survival Trust.

Published by

Geerings of Ashford Ltd.

Illustrations by Barbara Seth.

Photographs courtesy of Brake Bros. Foodservice Ltd. and Larderfresh.

ISBN 1 873953 18 6

Designed and printed by Geerings of Ashford Ltd
Cobbs Wood House, Chart Road, Ashford, Kent TN23 1EP.

Contents

	Page
The Rare Breeds Survival Trust	5
Pork	7
Lamb	47
Beef	69
Poultry	81

Registered Charity No. 269442

RARE BREEDS SURVIVAL TRUST
Conservation in Action

Current farming practice makes use of only a restricted number of breeds of farm livestock, while agricultural trends and breeding techniques limit even further the number of bloodlines used. This causes genetic material to be lost, and excludes many hardy and productive breeds from modern farming. Some of these breeds, for example British Saddleback pigs and Wensleydale sheep, were numerous less than 50 years ago. Yet by 1973, when the Rare Breeds Survival Trust was formed, their numbers had fallen so low that their continued existence could not be taken for granted.

Since its formation, the Trust has successfully reversed the trends of the previous century. Several breeds which were once seriously depleted are now out of danger and have left our list. Not one breed has been lost since the Trust started work.

Our farm animals are as important to the ecology of Great Britain as wild animals and flowers and they represent not only a vital part of our national heritage, but also a valuable resource for future commercial systems of production. As the only UK charity promoting and conserving endangered breeds of farm animals it is our responsibility to ensure that they are available for the benefit of future generations.

The Trust's activities include:

✦ Surveys and censuses of breed populations

✦ Blood-typing, DNA analyses and other scientific research

✦ Developing sound breeding policies and advising livestock owners

✦ Giving grants for the establishment and maintenance of breeding groups of animals

✦ Keeping animals from vulnerable bloodlines

✦ Maintaining vital genetic materials such as semen and embryos

✦ Providing information, registration facilities, advertising, shows and sales and workshops

✦ Educating and informing through the pages of our magazine, *the ARK*, illustrative posters, fact sheets and in the national press and with practical demonstrations

✦ Presentations to Government Departments and Ministers of State

How the Trust Operates

The Trust is governed by an elected Council, supported and advised by Committees on matters of management, breed activities and technical and scientific subjects.

Its headquarters is at the National Agricultural Centre, Kenilworth, where a permanent staff manages Trust affairs, and technical experts provide advice on genetics, animal health, livestock management and breed related topics.

The Trust's objectives and work are promoted at many agricultural shows each year, and the annual Show and Sale provides an opportunity for members to exhibit and sell livestock, contributing to the spread of valuable genetic qualities.

Members are kept in touch with the Trust's activities through the pages of its magazine, *the ARK*.

Membership subscriptions finance much of the Trust's work and there is an urgent need for sponsorship, grants, donations and bequests to enable it to further develop and increase its activities.

About this book

Many endangered breeds have not been subjected to the strong selection pressures prevalent in modern agriculture. They remain adapted to natural non-intensive systems of production which enhance even further the special quality of their products and their value in traditional recipes.

We are delighted to be associated with Geerings of Ashford Ltd in the production of this recipe book. It will help to promote the sale of meat from rare breeds, and will give encouragement to producers as more people become aware of the wonderful richness of traditional dishes.

Further information is available from

RARE BREEDS SURVIVAL TRUST
National Agricultural Centre
Kenilworth
Warwickshire CV8 2LG
Telephone 01203 696551

Pork Recipes

Night Before Breakfast

1 lb/454g spicy pork sausage

6 eggs

2 cups milk

4 slices of bread

1 cup strong cheese (grated)

Sauté sausage, drain and set aside. Beat eggs with milk and set aside. Cube the bread and layer bread cubes, sausage and grated cheese in a greased 9 by 13 baking dish. Pour the egg mixture on top. Refrigerate overnight. In the morning, bake at 350°C/180°F/gas mark 4 for 40-45 minutes.

Jan Palmer

Oklahoma, USA

Pigs' Feet a l'Anglaise

Pigs' feet

Cold water

Salt

Sage

1 large or 2 small onions

Pepper

English mustard

Flour

1 egg

Fresh white breadcrumbs

Take some well-cleansed pigs' feet and put them into a saucepan with enough cold water to cover them, season it with salt, bring it to the boil, skim it and boil on gently for 3½ to 4 hours. Then take up and when slightly cooled split the feet, remove the bones, and season inside with chopped sage and onion, and a little pepper and English mustard. Fold them up again and put to press between 2 plates with a weight on top. When cold take up and cut in strips about one inch wide; dip these into flour and then into whole beaten egg and freshly made white breadcrumbs, bat with the palette knife to make quite smooth, and then deep fry for about 5 minutes. Garnish with fried parsley and serve piping hot.

Nicky Guthrie

Inverness

Pork Brawn *(Fromage de Cochan)*

Take half of a pig's head and 2 pigs' feet that have been cleansed and then salted for 4 days, rinse them in cold water and put them into a saucepan with enough cold water to cover them. Bring to the boil, skim the water and allow it to simmer on the side of the stove for 4½ to 5 hours. Take up, remove all the bones from the head and the feet, and cut all up together in little square pieces and season with salt and pepper. Put into a brawn press (if you have one! If not, put it into a basin or charlotte mould) with about half a pint of the liquor in which the head was cooked, press it, and when cold turn out and garnish with picked green parsley.

From Mrs A B Marshall's Cookery Book, published 1885.

Nicky Guthrie
Inverness

Sausagemeat

1 lb/454g belly pork

5-6 oz/150g bread (soaked and squeezed)

Sage

Salt and pepper

A little nutmeg

Mince the pork or put through a processor, add the bread, sage, salt and pepper and nutmeg. Mix thoroughly.

Ann How
Market Harborough

Pork Chops in Cream

4 lean chops

1 ½ oz unsalted butter

½ lb chopped mushrooms

1 tbls lemon juice

¾ oz flour

Salt and pepper

1 tsp thyme (chopped)

2 tbls oil

4 tbls lightly whipped cream

1 tbls chopped parsley

Sauté chops till golden, not cooked through. Remove and keep warm. Drain off all but 2 tbls. fat in pan. Add mushrooms, cook, then add lemon, flour, salt, pepper and thyme. Arrange chops on buttered squares of foil and top with mushroom mix, cream and parsley. Seal parcels up and cook for 50 mins. at 175°C/335°F/gas mark 3½, serve with baked tomatoes and green salad.

Ann How
Market Harborough

Homemade Sausages

1 lb minced pork leanish off cuts

4 oz fresh brown breadcrumbs

1 level tsp salt and pepper to taste

½ level tsp dry mustard

1 level tsp mixed herbs, dry

3½ level tsps mixed herbs, fresh

4 tbls milk

Lard for frying

Mix all ingredients well, add milk. Mould into shape by piping or hand. Fry a few at a time turning until brown all over and cooked through.

Rosalind Ragg

Hungarian Pork

1 lb cubed, boneless pork. Shoulder is ideal.

1 lb chopped onions

8 ozs spicy pork sausage (Chorizo or similar) (Use a continental sausage with 100% meat, not an English 'Banger')

1 tbls oil

14 oz tin tomatoes

1 tsp Caraway seeds

1 dsp paprika

¼ pt sour cream and rings of red and green pepper to garnish

Fry the onions slowly in the oil until soft and very dark. Add the pork and toss until browned all over. Stir in the paprika and caraway seeds and cook for one minute before adding the tomatoes. Slice the sausage and add to the mixture. Bring to the boil and transfer to ovenproof casserole. Cook in a moderate oven for about one hour or until the meat is tender. Check the seasoning and just before serving swirl in the soured cream so that you have a marbled effect and top with pepper rings. Serve with noodles or small dumplings or very creamy mashed potatoes. Try stir fry cabbage with a few caraway seeds as a vegetable accompaniment.

Frances Kennedy

Shenstone

Heal Farm Roast Rare Breed Pork

3½ to 4lb Loin of Rare Breed Pork off the bone, finely scored and left flat (not rolled and tied)

Salt

Star Anise, optional

For the stuffing:

6 slices from a standard size loaf of either granary or white bread

1 large onion

Small handful of fresh sage

Salt and pepper

An assortment of vegetables to roast with the joint. Potatoes cut into quarters, halved onions, carrots sliced lengthwise and quartered parsnips are our standard additions. Serve with a green vegetable, apple purée and strong English mustard.

One hour before the joint is due to go into the oven, rub the scored pork rind well with salt, and allow to stand at room temperature, the salt will draw moisture from the skin. Dry and scatter with fresh salt, plus a little Star Anise, if liked.

Finely chop the onion and simmer in a little water, with a good pinch of salt and pepper, until tender.

Magimix the bread into coarse crumbs.

Rough chop the fresh sage.

Combine the crumbs, sage and onion adding enough of the onion cooking water to hold the mixture together.

Butter a large roasting tin and put the stuffing into one end so that it is at least ½ an inch thick. Place the pork on top of the stuffing, thick part towards the middle of the tin, leave about ½ an inch of stuffing showing around the edge, this will get crispy and brown. In the remaining part of the roasting tin arrange the vegetables, cut side down and season with salt and pepper.

Place in a pre heated oven, 425°F/220°C/Gas 7 or the roasting oven of an Aga. Cook for 25 minutes to the pound and 25 minutes over, a four pound joint will take approx. 2 hours and 5 minutes. Towards the end of the cooking time, test by pushing a skewer into the

Heal Farm Roast Rare Breed Pork (continued)

thickest part of the meat, if the juices run clear the joint is ready, if they are still pink, add a few more minutes to the cooking time. Baste the vegetables with the cooking juices at least once during cooking.

Remove the joint from the roasting tin to a large carving plate and leave to rest in a warm place for 15 minutes, this is essential to prevent excessive loss of juices when carving.

Carefully remove the roast vegetables to a serving dish, they should be brown and crispy on the underside and leave behind caramel with which to make gravy. If the pork is quite fat you may need to tip the tin slightly for a few seconds to let the fat drain away from the stuffing. Cut the stuffing into slices and arrange around the meat.

You should now be left with a fairly messy looking roasting tin, this is almost the best bit! Tip out the fat and put the tin onto a low heat, pour in half a pint or so of water or half and half water and dry cider, gently bring to simmering point all the time working away at unsticking the caramelized bits with a wooden spoon, when the tin is clean the gravy is ready, check the seasoning and pour the whole lot into a gravy boat.

Serve with green vegetables, apple purée and plenty of cold, dry cider.

Anne Petch

Tamworth Pork Fillets

1½-2 lbs pork fillet

1 tbls olive oil

2 oz butter

3 tbls apple juice

2 tbls apple jelly

¼ pt mixed yoghurt and cream

¼ tsp potato flour, arrowroot or cornflower

2-3 tsps pink or green peppercorns or a mixture of both

Salt and pepper

Trim the fillets. Cut on the slant into 1" wide slices, bat out gently under cling film and season when ready to cook. Stir in the potato flour with the yoghurt and cream so that it won't curdle when boiled. Heat the butter and oil in a large frying pan and when the frothing subsides sauté the medallions of pork briskly for 1-2 minutes on each side, remove to a serving dish. Add the apple juice and jelly to the pan and stir in any bits, then cool the pan before adding the yoghurt mixture and the peppercorns. Bring to the boil whisking well, simmer a moment, correct seasoning, pour over the pork.

Ann Wheatley-Hubbard
Boyton

Pigs Liver in Spicy Cream Sauce

1 lb pigs liver, very thinly sliced

2 small onions, chopped

1 oz peeled and grated ginger

6 cloves garlic, crushed

2 fresh chillies, seeded and chopped

½ tsp chilli powder

1 tsp cumin seeds

1 tsp garam masala

¼ pt tomato juice

¼ pt single cream

4 tbls melted butter

2 tbls fresh coriander, chopped

Heat the butter in a heavy pan and fry the onions until soft and dark brown. Add the garlic and ginger and cook for a further two minutes. Add the chillies, chilli powder, cumin seeds and garam masala and cook for a few seconds before adding the liver. Cook the liver for no more than 2 minutes. Do not overcook. Add the tomato juice to the pan and bring to the boil. Add the cream and stir well. Adjust the seasoning and serve sprinkled with fresh, chopped coriander.

This is a very rich dish so needs only a plain rice or bread to accompany. It is also a dish which many liver haters eat and enjoy.

Frances Kennedy
Shenstone

Wiltshire Plait

10 ozs lean end belly pork, boneless and de-rinded weight

Half a small cooking apple

2 ozs mature cheddar cheese

1 small onion

1 clove garlic

4-5 tbls chopped parsley

1 egg

Salt and pepper

Puff pastry made with 6 ozs flour

Mince the pork. Chop the onion, crush the garlic and cut the apple and cheese into small dice. Mix these ingredients together with the parsley and half the egg. Roll out the pastry to a 10 inch square. Pat the pork into a fat sausage shape and lay it down the centre of the pastry. Cut the pastry diagonally into 2" strips on either side of the pork mixture. Damp the end of each pastry strip, then fold the strips, alternately from each side, over the meat filling to create a lattice or plait effect. Seal the pastry ends and glaze with the remaining egg. Slide the plait onto a damp baking sheet and bake at 425°F/220°C/gas mark 7 for 20 mins. then at 350°F/180°C/gas mark 4 for a further 20-25 mins.

Frances Kennedy
Shenstone

Roast Pork Chinese Style

1½ lb belly pork

Marinade:

2 tbls light soy sauce

1 tbls soft brown sugar

1 tbls soya bean paste

2 tbls fruit sauce

2 tbls red wine

1 tbls oil

1 tsp sesame paste

1 shallot

1 clove garlic finely chopped

To finish:

1 tsp sesame oil

1 tbls honey

Remove the rind from the pork and cut into 3" strips. Mix all the marinade ingredients and leave the pork in this for at least an hour.

Heat the grill on high for 5 mins. and then reduce the heat, place the pork on a rack and grill for 25 mins., turning from time to time.

Mix the sesame oil and honey together and brush the pork. Grill for a further 10 minutes.

Slice the pork thickly, place on a hot dish and garnish with fresh pineapple. Serve with fried rice with prawns and a selection of fresh vegetables.

Frances Kennedy

Shenstone

Pork, Apple and Sesame Pie

1½ lbs thick end draught pork

1 sharp cooking apple

1 large onion

1 tbls chopped parsley

1 tbls toasted sesame seeds

1 or 2 large cloves garlic, crushed

1 large beaten egg

Mince the pork, not too finely. Peel, core and chop the apple, peel and finely chop the onion. Using your hands and a large mixing bowl, mix together all the ingredients and add salt and pepper.

Leave to stand in a cool place for a couple of hours or overnight to allow the flavours to blend. (This does make a big difference to the final taste).

Line a dish or tin with short crust pastry and fill with pork mixture.

Top with the same pastry or puff. Bake in a moderate oven. The time taken will depend on the depth of the pie. About an hour will probably do.

This is also very nice with the addition of about 4 ozs of strong cheese to the pork mixture.

Frances Kennedy
Shenstone

Pork in Puff Pastry

1¾ lb boned loin of pork

Salt and pepper

½ tsp brown sugar

1 tsp juniper berries, crushed

1 pt boiling vegetable stock

1 lb frozen puff pastry (thawed)

1 egg, beaten

2 tbls tomato purée

8 fl oz single cream

This is a wonderful juicy way of serving pork. You will find the juniper berries give the dish a lovely flavour.

Heat oven to 190°C/375°F/gas mark 5. Place meat in roasting tin, rub with pepper, sugar and juniper berries. Roast for 10 minutes. Pour stock over meat and roast for further 40 minutes basting occasionally. Allow meat to cool in juices.

Roll out ¾ of pastry to an oblong (about 12" x 10"). Brush edges with little beaten egg and place the meat in the centre. Wrap pastry around the meat and press edges to seal. Brush with beaten egg.

Decorate with remaining pastry, brush with egg and chill for 30 minutes. Heat oven to 220°C/425°F/gas mark 7. Place meat on baking tray and bake for 35 mins. Lower oven temperature to 180°C/350°F/gas mark 4. Cook for further 10 mins.

Heat meat juices to boiling point. Stir in tomato purée and cream, season and strain before serving with pork.

Serve with baked potatoes and mixed salad with herb dressing.

(Serves 4)

Bronwen Watts
Swansea

Faggots

1 ½ lbs pigs liver (remove gristle and skin)

1 lb belly pork

1 large onion, finely chopped

4 oz fresh breadcrumbs

Stock

Salt, pepper and 2 tsps dried sage

Mince liver and pork. Add breadcrumbs, sage and seasoning. Form into balls using well floured hands. Place close together in roasting tin. Add stock to come halfway up the faggots. Bake in moderate oven for 45 mins. until nicely browned.

Traditionally served with 'mushy' peas (tinned processed peas).

Bronwen Watts

Swansea

Saveloys

6 lbs pork

1 lb common salt

1 oz salt petre

3 tsps pepper

12 sage leaves

1 lb breadcrumbs

Salt the pork, after removing the skin and bone, using both the common salt and salt petre, and let it remain in the pickle for 3 days. Then mince it up very fine and season it with pepper and the 12 sage leaves, chopped as small as possible. Add the grated bread and mix all well together, fill the skins and bake in a slow oven for ½ hour.

Olwen Fussell
Cambridge

Gloucestershire Pickled Tongue

8¾ pints water

2¾ lb coarse salt

1 oz salt petre

8 oz black treacle

1 lb 2 oz natural dark soft brown sugar

The secret of good pickled tongue lies in the treacle.

Put all the ingredients together in a large pan bringing slowly to the boil and boil for 3 minutes stirring occasionally. Skim the scum from the top. Leave the liquid to cool then pour into a sterilized container.

Make absolutely sure any tongues you wish to preserve are as fresh as possible.

Sterilize a large needle by holding it over a candle flame or under boiling water and prick the tongues thoroughly all over, re-sterilizing the needle frequently.

Immerse the tongues in the pickle and cover them with a scalded board so that they are kept below the level of the liquid. Turn the tongues and stir the pickle occasionally. Large ones such as ox tongues should be cured for 3 weeks, sheeps and pig tongues for 1 week.

To cook the tongues, simmer them in a good rich stock until they are tender allowing about 1 hour to each 1lb. Drain them, reserving the stock and press them overnight.

Put them into a shallow dish. Heat the stock which will have set into a jelly, allow it just to cool without setting again and pour it over the tongues. Cover and store in the refrigerator.

Olwen Fussell
Cambridge

Pork Hams (Hannah Glasse 1747)

You must take a fat hind-quarter of pork, and cut off a fine ham. Take an ounce of saltpetre, a pound of coarse sugar, and a pound of common salt; mix altogether, and rub it well. Let it lie a month in this pickle, turning and basting it every day, then hang it in wood-smoke as you do your beef, in a dry place, so as no heat comes to it; and if you keep them long, hang them for a month or two in a damp place, so as they will be mouldy, and it will make them cut fine and short. Never lay these hams in water till you boil them, and then boil them in a copper, if you have one, or the biggest pot you have. Put them in the cold water, and let them be four or five hours before they boil. Skim the pot well and often, till it boils. If it is a very large one, two hours will boil it; if a small one, an hour and a half will do, provided it be a great while before the water boils. Take it up half an hour before dinner, pull off the skin, and throw raspings finely sifted all over. Hold a red-hot fire shovel over it, and when dinner's ready take a few raspings in a sieve and sift all over the dish; then lay in your ham, and with your finger make fine figures round the edge of the dish. Be sure to boil your ham in as much water as you can, and to keep it skimming all the time till it boils. It must be at least four hours before it boils.

When you broil any of these hams in slices or bacon, have some boiling water ready, and let the slices lie a minute or two in the water; then broil them, it takes out the salt, and makes them eat finer.

Timothy & Anne Wilson
Harwell

Ginger Pig Casserole

Tamworth cubed pork

Onion

Seasoned flour

Orange juice

Seasoning

Roll the pork in seasoned flour and brown on all sides. Place in a casserole dish and fry the onions gently. Put the onions with the pork in the casserole dish and wash out the pan with orange juice. Add to the casserole and top up with orange juice if necessary. Cook at 180°C/350°F/gas mark 4 for 1 hour.

Caroline Wheatley-Hubbard

Boyton

Porc Cacciatore

Tamworth cubed pork

Onion

Garlic

Red pepper

Tomato

Tomato purée

Stock

Roll the pork in seasoned flour and brown on all sides. Put in a casserole and fry the onions, red peppers and garlic gently. When these are soft add the tomatoes and tomato purée and cook gently for another five minutes. Add the sauce to the pork and top up with stock if necessary. Cook at 180°C/350°F/gas mark 4 for one hour.

Caroline Wheatley-Hubbard
Boyton

Tamworth Sausages

10 lb Tamworth belly pork and trimmings (meat from the head, and also the tongue)

2 pints water

1 lb rusk - ask any butcher who makes his own sausages if you can buy some from him

3 tbls salt

3 tbls pepper

Sausage skins - again, ask your butcher

Mince all the meats together. Put the rusk, salt and pepper, and other herbs and spices you might like to add into a plastic bag and shake them all up thoroughly. Sprinkle over the minced meats and then mix in (fingers work best!). Add the water and mix again. Let this mixture stand for about an hour.

Mince the mixture again before you fill the skins. On most machines this is all one process. Twist the sausages (if you are quick you can do this as you are filling the skins!), then leave them to set in a cool place preferably overnight before packing and freezing.

Remember: there are no preservatives in these sausages and they should be frozen as soon as possible and not left for too long in the fridge either before or after freezing.

This is a base recipe and there are lots of different spices and herbs which you can add: try garlic, all spice, sage, mace, in different quantities and invent your own secret recipe!

Caroline Wheatley-Hubbard
Boyton

Tamworth Tenderloin Wheels

2 Tamworth pork tenderloins

Tamworth pork sausagemeat

Streaky Tamworth bacon

Wine

Seasoning

Split the tenderloins in two down the centre to make two long strips. Bash the strips. Lay sausagemeat along the strips and roll each strip up. Cover the outside with bashed streaky bacon and hold in place with a toothpick (or two).

Brown the rolls all over in a casserole dish on the top of the stove. Add wine to a depth of less than 1" and cover. Cook in a hot oven 190°C/375°F/gas mark 5 for approx. 25 minutes (depending on the size of the tenderloins). Carve or serve with the remaining cooking juices.

(Serves 4)

Caroline Wheatley-Hubbard
Boyton

Raised Pork Pie

3-4 small veal bones

2 small onions

1 bay leaf

6 peppercorns

2 lb boneless leg or shoulder of Tamworth pork or 1 lb pork with 1 lb bacon

¼ tsp cayenne pepper

¼ tsp ground mace

¼ tsp ground ginger

¼ tsp ground sage

¼ tsp ground marjoram

Salt and pepper

Grease and line an 8 inch spring release cake tin with greaseproof paper. Boil the bones, onion, bay leaf and peppercorns for 20 minutes, or longer until the liquid is reduced to ¼ pint, strain and leave to cool.

Make your pastry.

Continues overleaf

Raised Pork Pie (continued)

Hot water crust pastry:

1 lb plain flour

2 tsps salt

4 oz lard or lard/butter

9 fl oz water

Egg to glaze

The art is to work fast. Mix the flour and salt together and make a well in the middle. Into this pour the lard boiling in 9 fl oz of water, beat with a wooden spoon to form a fairly soft dough. Pinch this lightly together and knead until smooth and silky. Cover with cling film or a damp cloth and leave for 20-30 minutes in a warm place. Do not allow to cool and harden.

Cut the pork into cubes and mix with the spices and herbs, 3 tsps salt and pepper to taste. Line the tin with ⅔ of the pastry and spoon in the mixture with 4 tbls of the cool stock. Cover with the remaining pastry and brush with beaten egg. Bake at 220°C/425°F/gas mark 7 for 30 minutes, and then reduce the oven temperature to 180°C/350°F/gas mark 4 and bake for a further 2½ hours. Leave to cool in the tin for two hours and then chill overnight. Warm the jellied stock to liquefy and pour into the centre of the pie. Chill for another hour to set before serving.

Caroline Wheatley-Hubbard
Boyton

Pork and Herb Paté

8 oz streaky bacon rashers

1 medium onion

8 oz pigs' liver

1 lb belly pork (rinded and some fat removed)

Salt and freshly ground pepper

2 tsp fresh sage or 1 tsp dried sage

1 tbls fresh marjoram or 1 tsp dried

1 tbls fresh parsley

½ tsp mace

Trim and stretch the bacon and line a 1 lb loaf tin. In a food processor mix the onion, liver, belly pork, herbs, mace, salt and pepper. Press this mixture into the lined loaf tin, cover tightly with foil and bake in a bain marie at 180°C/350°F/gas mark 4 for about 2 hours or until the juices run clear. Remove from the bain marie and place heavy weights on top of the foil covering until cold. Chill and refrigerate overnight before turning out.

Caroline Wheatley-Hubbard
Boyton

Stuffed Cabbage Rolls

2 tbls vegetable oil

1 medium onion, finely chopped

1 tsp chilli powder

12 oz minced pork

8 oz can of tomatoes

Salt and pepper

10 oz can red kidney beans

16 large Savoy cabbage leaves

¾ pint cheese sauce

2 oz cheddar cheese

Pinch of cayenne or paprika

Fry the onion gently for about 5 minutes, sprinkle in the chilli powder and fry for another 1-2 minutes. Add the pork and fry until brown, add the tomatoes and bring to the boil, add salt and pepper and simmer for 20 minutes stirring occasionally, add the kidney beans and remove from the heat.

Blanch the cabbage leaves for 3 minutes, 4 at a time, rinse and dry with kitchen towel. Cut out the central stalk and fill the stalk end of each leaf with 1-1½ tbls mixture. Fold in the sides and make a parcel. Put in a baking dish seam side down, cover with cheese sauce and bake in the oven at 180°C/350°F/gas mark 4 for 30 minutes. Sprinkle with cheese and cayenne or paprika and grill for 5 minutes before serving. Serve with boiled rice.

Caroline Wheatley-Hubbard
Boyton

Chilli Pork and Beans

2 tbls vegetable oil

2 lb pork shoulder cut in cubes

1 large onion, roughly chopped

2 celery sticks, sliced

1-2 crushed garlic cloves

6 oz red kidney beans, soaked

1 tbls black treacle

1 tbls French mustard

1 tsp chilli powder

Salt and pepper

Fry the cubes of meat on all sides, removing when brown with a slotted spoon. Fry the onion, celery and garlic for 10 minutes. Add the drained kidney beans and 2 pints of water and boil for 10 minutes, add the pork, treacle, mustard, chilli and pepper to taste and cook in a casserole for 3 hours at 150°C/300°F/gas mark 4, stirring occasionally. Add a little salt halfway through, and more water if dry.

Serve with boiled rice. A bowl of natural yoghurt can also be served to cool the palate.

Caroline Wheatley-Hubbard
Boyton

Normandy Pork

8 Tamworth pork chops, trimmed

1 tbls plain flour

Salt and pepper

2 oz butter

2 tbls olive oil

½ pint dry French cider

2 tbls finely chopped parsley

3 crisp eating apples

3 tbls brandy

4 tbls double cream

Coat the chops in seasoned flour and fry in the butter and oil until browned. Return all the chops to the pan and pour in the cider and add the parsley. Simmer for 30-40 minutes until tender. Arrange on a dish and keep hot under foil. Slice the apples without peeling and fry in the rest of the butter and oil. Heat the brandy while adding the apple slices round the casserole then pour over the apple slices. Heat the cooking liquid, add the cream and pour over the chops.

Caroline Wheatley-Hubbard
Boyton

Tamworth Pork Chops en Croute

2 tbls vegetable oil

½ oz magarine

4 Tamworth loin chops

4 tsps chopped fresh sage

Salt and ground pepper

6 tbls dry white wine or chicken stock

4 tbls redcurrant jelly

14 oz packet puff pastry

Beaten egg to glaze

Brown the chops on both sides, lower the heat and sprinkle on the seasoning, pour over the liquid and simmer for 20 minutes or until tender, basting and turning once.

Remove the chops, stir some of the jelly into the juices and reduce. Roll out the pastry, cut into four and place a chop in the middle of each with a little of the jelly mixture. Wrap the pastry round the chop, seal the ends with water and brush with beaten egg.

Bake in the oven for 20 minutes at 220°C/425°F/gas mark 7 and serve with the remaining redcurrant jelly mixture.

Caroline Wheatley-Hubbard
Boyton

Cider Pork Sauté

1 lb green dessert apples

1 lb floury old potatoes

Salt and pepper

2 oz butter

½ pint dry cider

2 tbls capers

1 lb Tamworth pork escalope

1 tbls vegetable oil

1 small onion, chopped

1 tbls plain flour

Beaten egg to glaze

Peel half the apples, halve and core; peel and cut into chunks the potatoes. Cook in a saucepan of salted water for 20 mins. Press through a sieve into a bowl and beat in 1 oz of the butter, add the salt and pepper to taste, spoon or pipe this mixture at either end of a shallow ovenproof dish.

Cut the escalope into fine strips, quarter and core the remaining apples and slice into a bowl of cold water. Fry the pork strips a few at a time until browned, add the onion and fry, return the pork and add in the flour, cook for a few minutes then blend in the cider and bring to the boil. Drain the apple and simmer gently for 4-5 minutes. Stir in the capers, salt and pepper and put in the centre of the dish. Brush the potato with beaten egg and bake at 200°C/400°F/gas mark 6 for 25-30 minutes.

Caroline Wheatley-Hubbard

Boyton

Noisettes de Porc Touraine

12-16 large plump prunes

½ pint dry white wine

1½ lb Tamworth pork tenderloin

1½ tbls plain flour

Salt and pepper

1 oz butter

1 tbls redcurrant jelly

1 tbls olive oil

2 tbls port

¼ pint double cream

Soak the prunes in wine overnight. Cut the fillet into ¼ inch slices and bat out between paper, coat with seasoned flour and fry till golden brown, drain on kitchen paper. Simmer the prunes in the wine for 20 minutes, then add the pork and simmer for 10 minutes. Arrange in a dish with the prunes round the edge and keep warm. Stir the port and jelly into the cooking liquid and boil to reduce. Lower the heat, stir in the cream and heat gently. Adjust the seasoning and drizzle over the pork.

Caroline Wheatley-Hubbard
Boyton

Sausage Balls

1 lb sausage

1 lb sharp cheddar cheese, grated

3½ cups biscuit mix

**Optional: 1 tbls Worcestershire sauce,
   ⅛ tsp cayenne pepper**

Combine all ingredients with hands. Shape loosely into small balls. Bake at 180°C/350°F/gas mark 4 for 15-20 minutes. Makes 100 snack sized balls.

Jan Palmer
Oklahoma, USA

Sweet & Sour Gammon Rasher

4 rashers

1 tbls butter

4 tbls vinegar (raspberry if available)

2 tbls redcurrant jelly

2 tsps made mustard (English)

2 tsps paprika

2 tbls soft brown sugar

Fry gammon in butter till cooked, remove, and make remaining ingredients into a sauce.

Ann How
Market Harborough

John Whitley's Cured Ham

1 leg pork (14 lbs)

1 oz sugar

1 lb salt

½ oz pepper

1 oz salt petre (pounded)

Sprinkle pepper all over meat - mix other ingredients - lay pork in tub and rub them well into it. Let it lie 18 to 20 days rubbing it once daily. Wash well and dry on a rough cloth, sprinkle with flour and hang in a draughty place until dry. It should be kept at least 4 months before good to eat.

Miss A W Mason

East Wellow

Mrs Hiscock's 2 Hams

2 quarts/4 pints of strong beer

1 lb bay salt

1 lb brown sugar

¼ lb salt petre

1 lb common salt

Boil together and pour over the hams as hot as you can bear your finger in. Keep in pickle for 3 weeks.

Olwen Fussell

Cambridge

Coarse French Paté

8 oz streaky Tamworth bacon

½ pint milk

Few slices of onion

Bay leaf

Peppercorns

1 or 2 cloves

1 oz butter or marge

¾ oz plain flour

1 lb Tamworth belly pork

1 lb pig's liver

1 small onion, quartered

2 garlic cloves

2 tbsp dry vermouth

Salt, pepper and oil

Trim and stretch the bacon and line the container. Put the milk and flavouring ingredients in a saucepan and bring slowly to the boil, cover and leave for 15 mins. Strain the milk and use to make a white sauce, cover and leave to cool. Chop the meats and onion in a food processor, add the garlic, vermouth, salt and pepper and beat in the white sauce. Spoon into dish, cover with foil and bake in a bain marie at 180°C/350°F/gas mark 4 for about 2¼ hours.

Caroline Wheatley-Hubbard
Boyton

Bacon Hot Pot

1½ lb collar or slipper

2 lb potatoes

1 small onion, skinned and thinly sliced

2 cooking apples, peeled, cored and thickly sliced

2 tsp chopped fresh sage or 1 tsp dried

Salt and pepper

¼ pt unsweetened natural apple juice

¼ pt water

½ oz unsalted butter

1 tbsp vegetable oil

Remove the rind and excess fat from the bacon and cut into bite-sized pieces. Put into a saucepan, cover with cold water and bring to the boil. Drain thoroughly. Peel the potatoes and slice thinly, using a mandolin slicer if available. Put bacon, potatoes, onion and apples in a shallow oven proof casserole, sprinkle each layer with sage and seasoning to taste as you go. (Take care not to add too much salt). Finish with a layer of potatoes. Mix together the apple juice and water and pour slowly into the casserole. Cover and cook in the oven at 180°C/350°F/gas mark 4 for 1½ hours. Melt the butter with the oil in a pan, uncover the casserole and brush the top with the melted fat. Return to the oven and cook uncovered for 30 minutes or until golden brown. Serve hot.

Caroline Wheatley-Hubbard
Boyton

Peanut Glazed Bacon Hock

2½ lb bacon hock

1 medium carrot, peeled and sliced

1 medium onion, skinned and quartered

1 bay leaf

2 tbls lemon marmalade

2 tbls demerara sugar

2 tsps lemon juice

Dash of Worcestershire sauce

1 oz salted peanuts, chopped

Put bacon in a casserole with carrot, onion and bay leaf. Pour enough water to come halfway up the joint, cover and cook in the oven at 180°C/350°F/gas mark 4 for about 2¼ hours. Remove bacon from casserole carefully, cut off and discard the rind, score the fat. Put the marmalade, sugar, lemon juice and worcestershire sauce in a bowl and mix well. Place the joint in a roasting tin, spread the mixture over the surface of the joint and sprinkle on the chopped nuts. Increase the oven temperature to 220°C/425°F/gas mark 7 and cook for 15 minutes to glaze. Serve sliced.

(Serves 6)

Caroline Wheatley-Hubbard
Boyton

Lamb Recipes

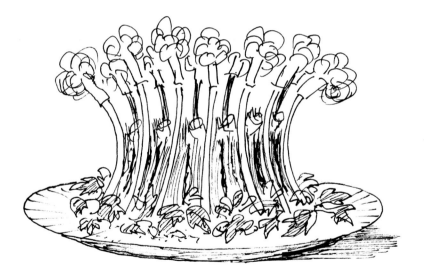

Shupouro (Origin Mongolia)

For the Tare sauce:

220cc Japanese Soya sauce

220cc Japanese sake

100cc Mirin (sweet sake)

1 leek (chopped)

40g fresh ginger (chopped)

25g garlic (chopped)

70cc vinegar

35cc sesame oil

Chopped parsley

To make the sauce mix all the ingredients thoroughly and serve cold.

For the stew:

2 kgs lamb pieces (neck & lower parts of the legs)

300g negi (this is a kind of onion like a cross between a leek and a spring onion - either should suffice)

150g fresh ginger

2.5ltr water

60g salt

Use the neck and lower parts of the legs. These are chopped into pieces and just covered with water in a pan. Add long sections of "negi" and coarsely chopped fresh ginger (including the skin).

Bring gently to the boil and add salt, a little at a time, and keep tasting until too salty (don't worry, the liquor will be thrown away eventually). Continue to boil covered with a lid for two hours. From time to time take off the scum. Now ready to eat and serve the meat that picks off from the bones to each person, and dip it in "tare" sauce.

Enjoy the meat of the four-horned Manx Loghtan, or the two-horned Hebridean, cooked this way.

Tadaka Momose
Japan

Raw Lamb

Primitive breeds, with tasty flesh and little fat, will lend themselves perfectly to make this delicacy. To prepare, take the fresh fillet of loin and place in the freezer for a short while until firm (not frozen). Then slice thinly and lay out on a dish. Sprinkle with salt, pepper, olive oil and some rosemary.

The North Ronaldsay lamb should be ideal with its special seaweed flavour. In the southern Japanese island of Okinawa the people traditionally prepare young goats' meat.

Tadaka Momose
Japan

Stuffed Breast of Lamb

A large breast of lamb (or several smaller ones)

50g (2oz) fresh breadcrumbs

Grated rind of half a lemon

One-quarter of a whole nutmeg, grated

1 tbls freshly-chopped mint

1 tbls freshly-chopped parsley

1 tsp finely crushed rosemary

4 shallots (or 1 medium onion), finely chopped

1 small egg, beaten

Salt and black pepper

Pre-heat oven to 350°F/180°C/gas mark 4.

Put the breadcrumbs, shallots, mint, parsley, nutmeg, rosemary and lemon rind in a mixing bowl and season well with the salt and black pepper. Mix thoroughly and then stir in the egg to bind the mixture.

Lay out the lamb breast on a board: if the bones have not been removed use a sharp knife to cut them out, but without cutting through the meat. When all the bones have been removed spread the stuffing mixture evenly over the breast. Roll it up gently and not too tightly, tucking the free end over to prevent the stuffing falling out. (If using several smaller breasts, spread the stuffing evenly over all of them and roll them together to form a single roll). Tie securely, but not too tightly, in three places with string.

Wrap the meat in foil, place in a roasting tin and cook for 1½ hours. Then unwrap the foil, baste the meat with the juices and return to the oven for 30 mins to brown.

To serve cut the meat into thick slices: provide a thin gravy made from the pan juices. Redcurrant or crab apple jelly are good accompaniments.

Alyson & Richard Small
Carr Cross Hebrideans

Whitefaced Hot Pot

½ breast of lamb

Mint sauce

Good handful frozen peas

1 med. size parsnip

1 carrot

2 leeks

1 lb potatoes

Cook breast of lamb slowly. (Either overnight in slow cooker or stewed for 2 hours). Allow to become cold. Reserve ½ pint stock, discard bones and fat etc.

Place meat in base of large casserole and sprinkle generously with mint sauce. Prepare carrot, parsnip and leek, and cut into small pieces. Place on top of meat. Add the peas.

Prepare potatoes and slice thinly. Spread evenly on top of vegetables.

Bring stock to the boil and thicken with favourite browning. Pour over casserole. Cook, covered for ¾ hr at 200°C/400°F/gas mark 6. Remove cover and cook for approx. another ¾ hr until potatoes cooked, crisp and brown.

(Note: if you prefer 'large' chunks of vegetables it is best to microwave them on 'high' for 5 minutes before adding to the casserole).

(Serves 2)

Colin & Jill Jackson
Brent Broughton

Simple Soay

Whole leg of Soay lamb

Onion, peeled and sliced

Olive oil

Salt

Black pepper

Tomatoes, sliced

Parsley

Prepare a bed of sliced onions in a roasting dish. The bed should be sufficient for the leg to lie on. Place the leg on the bed of onion. Paint the exposed area of the leg with olive oil (a pastry brush is helpful to get a good but not excessive covering). A good grinding of salt and black pepper and then place slices of tomato over the lamb overlapping to provide a good covering. Sprinkle a good helping of chopped parsley over the tomatoes. Place in pre-heated oven and cook according to your preferred method. (See below).

Background and comments

The leg used was from Norwood Farm, Bath Road, Norton St Philip and weighed 2lb 13oz The leg was put in an oven pre-heated to 230°C/450°F/gas mark 8 for 10 minutes and then for a further 60 minutes at 180°C/350°F/gas mark 4*. All ovens and tastes vary so do not follow these times slavishly. Use the temperature settings and times that you prefer.

This size leg is sufficient for four adults.

*This equates to 26 minutes per lb and 15 over.

Serve with mint sauce and new potatoes. (The onions can be eaten but might be better added to a soup stock or casserole).

Iain Forbes
Bradford on Avon

Wensleydale in Beer

1½ - 2 lb (¾ kg - 1 kg) cubed meat with fat removed.

Use shoulder or trimmings from other joints; add heart, kidneys.

1 lb - 1½ lb (½ kg - ¾ kg) vegetables in season: parsnip, carrot, Jerusalem Artichokes, onions, shallots. Slice or cube.

Use 1 part water stock to 2 parts beer (or lager) to cover meat and vegetables in a SLOW COOKER. Refer to manufacturers instructions as this usually means starting off in a large saucepan.

Add garlic freshly diced, salt and black pepper to taste. Add herbs basil or rosemary to taste.

Cook for 7 hours in slow cooker, thickening with gravy granules or other thickener during last few minutes. Serve with mashed potatoes and your favourite greens.

Mrs S D Brunt
East Bridgford

Wensleydale Hogget Chops

Chops

Oil for cooking

Cardamom seeds

Fresh lovage leaves

Pinch salt

Beer or lager (75% with water if preferred)

As they are slow-growing animals, the Wensleydale mature lamb, quite large at 12-15 months, is particularly suitable for this dish; an early summer speciality!

Firstly, brown both sides of the chops in a little oil in a frying pan, then transfer them to a casserole dish. Add a few freshly-crushed green cardamom seeds, some fresh lovage leaves, a pinch of salt and nearly cover chops with beer or lager (75% with water if preferred). Cover dish with lid or foil. Bring to simmer, then cook at 180°C/350°F/gas mark 4 for 30-40 minutes.

Serve with mashed potatoes and green leaf vegetables; thickening the casserole juices with cornflour for gravy.

Mrs S D Brunt
East Bridgford

Wensleydale Roast Shoulder

The dark red flesh will be lightly covered with fat which conserves juices during the SLOW ROAST. Rub salt in the dry skin/outer fat to enhance crispness and flavour. More strongly flavoured than lamb, this joint can take a more pungent herb such as sage or basil, as well as the traditional rosemary. Place fresh or dried herbs between "layers" of meat. Cover with foil and slow cook at 175°C/350°F/gas mark 4 for 35 minutes per lb plus 35 minutes over. Remove foil half an hour before serving; the meat will be tender and tasty.

Serve with rhubarb sauce: simply cook a few sticks of rhubarb (from frozen is fine) in a little water until mushy, no sugar added.

Enjoy with a red wine such as Cabernet Sauvignon; mashed potatoes, sautéed parsnips, carrots and brussel tops; a little gravy made from meat juices.

Mrs S D Brunt
East Bridgford

Cotswold Mutton

Top half leg mature Cotswold wether - approx 4 lbs

3 onions

3 carrots

3 sticks celery

3 wineglasses of a solid red Burgundy

4 dessertspoons redcurrant jelly

¼ pint sour cream

3 bayleaves

Sprig thyme

Seasoning

Peel and dice vegetables and place in bottom of a casserole. Place meat, seasoning, bay leaves and thyme on top and add wine. Cover tightly and cook in moderate oven - 20 minutes per pound. When meat is cooked, put in a serving dish in the oven to keep it warm and strain juice into a saucepan. Bring to the boil and simmer for 5 minutes. Remove from heat and stir in redcurrant jelly and sour cream. Serve the sauce with the meat in a separate dish.

Lord Barber of Tewkesbury
Gotherington, Gloucestershire

Butterflied Southdown

5 lb leg of Southdown lamb (boned)

4 tbls olive oil

Fresh rosemary

Crushed garlic

Salt & pepper

Slice open the lamb and lay it flat on a chopping board. Make deep gashes in the thickest part of the lamb and open these out to give a more even piece of meat. Take four long skewers and push them through the lamb from side to side and the remaining two from top to bottom. Crush the garlic and rosemary and mix with the oil. Season the meat well and brush with a little seasoned oil. Leave to stand for about 30 minutes before cooking. Light the barbecue and when the coals are hot grill the lamb for 20-30 minutes each side, turning every 10 minutes and basting with the seasoned oil. When the lamb is cooked to your liking, place on a carving board and leave to rest for 15 minutes before removing the skewers and carving.

The lamb could be cooked in the oven at 200°C/400°F/gas mark 6 for the same length of time, but it is much more flavoursome if barbecued.

Mrs Jennifer Clare
Stainton, Nr. Kendal

Mango Stuffed Lamb

4-4½ lbs boned leg or shoulder of lamb

For the stuffing:

1 fresh mango, not too ripe

2 ozs plain cashew nuts, roughly chopped

2 cloves garlic, finely chopped

1 egg, lightly beaten

3-5 pinches of Cayenne Pepper

Well beforehand lay boned lamb out and, if necessary, cut pockets to receive the stuffing. Rub the meat all over with lemon juice and olive oil. Set aside in the fridge whilst you make the stuffing.

Prepare the mango. Easiest way and least messy: stand the fruit on its end, and with a sharp knife, cut down either side of the pip in the middle which gives two 'cheeks'. Lay the cheeks down and cut through almost to the skin, turn it inside out and you can detatch the flesh very easily and chop up the squares a bit more. Then move the knife under the remaining skin still on the pip and pare the flesh off the pip. Put all the chopped flesh and the other ingredients into a bowl. Mix well. Spoon it into the pockets, roll up the meat neatly and either tie with string or secure with skewers. Rub the joint with olive oil and salt. Cover it and leave for several hours - or overnight, in the fridge.

Finally take out and leave at room temperature for an hour before cooking, to bring out the flavour. Cook at 325°F/178°C/gas mark 3 in preheated oven for 1½ hours if you like it slightly pink. Longer for well done. You can add a wine glass of fresh orange juice to the gravy round the meat if you like.

Mrs W E Blunt

Firbank, Nr. Sedbergh

Castlemilk Bourguinonne

Cut leg or shoulder into 1-2" cubes discarding fat. Flour lightly and fry quickly in hot dripping, turning them until sealed and just brown.

Transfer to saucepan or casserole. Add salt and pepper, crushed garlic and thyme (preferably fresh). If using lamb, add peeled pickling onions.

Add red wine to cover, bring to boil and simmer in oven for 1½ hours. Add button mushrooms. Add flour cooked in fat used for frying meat and boil until thickened. Adjust seasoning.

Mature meat is excellent, but is best fried and cooked in red wine and seasoning for a preliminary 1½ hours before adding onions. Cook for a further hour then add mushrooms etc. as for lamb. This improves with resting therefore, is best made the day before.

Mrs Bridget Parke
Calne

Roast Saddle of Castlemilk

Roast in casserole roaster with a little water, rosemary, and plenty of dripping, then cook in oven with the lid on. This keeps the lean meat moist.

Saddle of lamb or shearling (very best): If possible get your slaughterer to do this as it's a tedious job requiring patience and a very sharp knife: if the skin is nicked along the backbone, juices will run out. The saddle should be boned out carefully after taking off legs and shoulders but leaving the breasts on (the breasts alone should be skinned if possible).

Make thyme and parsley stuffing with lemon juice, grated rind of lemon, lamb dripping, breadcrumbs and finely chopped onion.

Cut kidneys in thin slices and place along side of eye meat; put stuffing down both sides, wrap breasts round stuffing and tie up into delicious easily carved joint.

Roast in casserole roaster at 400°F/200°C/gas mark 6 for half an hour, then 200°F/100°C/gas mark ½ for one hour.

Mrs Bridget Parke

Calne

Primitive Pot Roast

Animals best killed May to August after spring grass; rams' meat not too strong.

Rub salt and pepper on top of joint.

Push clove of garlic between bone and flesh of narrow end of leg; squeeze garlic over shoulder.

Place joint in casserole roaster.

Prepare onions and a variety of root vegetables (carrots, swedes, turnips, artichokes etc.) - roughly cut and place round joint.

Add 1 pint of water, a little dripping on the top of the joint and herbs (parsley and stalks, thyme, mint etc.)

Put lid on casserole, cook in preheated oven at 400°F/200°C/gas mark 6 for ¾ hour then reduce temperature to 250°F/130°C/gas mark 1 for a further 2½ hours.

Carve and serve - delicious and tender!

Mrs Bridget Parke
Calne

Smoked Mutton

Pickle:

4lb cooking salt

1lb brown sugar

2oz salt petre

2oz peppercorns

2oz root ginger (or ground)

Few bay leaves

Suitable for leg or shoulder of mature lamb or shearling

Put all ingredients in 2 gallons of water and boil for 15 minutes. Cool. Rub joint with salt. Leave 24 hours. Place joint in suitable container. Cover with pickle. Put weight on top of meat to hold under pickle. Leave in cool place for 4-6 weeks according to age of sheep. Take out of pickle and take to friendly smoke house to be smoked for ½ a day.

Delicious carved very thinly like "Palma Ham". Keeps well.

Mrs Bridget Parke
Calne

Poached Mutton

1 leg of Rare Breed Mutton (Southdown for preference)

1 small onion stuck with 2 cloves

2 bay leaves

1 stick celery cut into pieces

Lamb or mutton stock

2 large carrots per person

Calculate the cooking time at 30 minutes to the pound. Put the meat and all the vegetables, except the carrots into a big pan with enough stock to cover the meat. Bring to the boil and reduce immediately to a simmer. Taste and add salt at this point if the stock is only lightly salted.

Start the cooking time from now. Half an hour before the meat will be ready add the scrubbed carrots to the pot. Remove the pan from the heat and put the meat on a board to stand for 15 minutes. Leave the carrots in the stock, off the heat.

Carve the mutton and serve with the carrots and a little of the stock to moisten. Check the seasoning at this point.

(This recipe was used for a regional final in the 1994 "Taste of Britain" competition).

Frances Kennedy
Shenstone

Lulu's Lamb

2 ozs butter

1 tsp caster sugar

3 cloves garlic

½ tsp Garam Masala

1 tsp ground cumin

½-1 tsp chilli powder

1 tsp ground coriander

1 fresh chilli, de-seeded and chopped

½ tsp salt

¼ pt double cream

Lemon juice to taste

1 lb leg of lamb, cut into 1" cubes

1 lb tomatoes, quartered

1 oz fresh ginger, grated

1 tsp cumin seeds

Melt 1 oz of the butter in a small heavy based pan. Add the tomatoes and sugar and bring to the boil. Stir and reduce to a simmer. Cover the pan with a folded tea towel and the lid. Steam cook for 5 minutes or until the tomatoes have collapsed.

Rub the tomatoes through a sieve to remove the skin and pips.

In a large pan melt the remaining butter and add the ginger and crushed garlic and fry until a pale golden colour. Do not allow to get too dark - it will spoil the colour of the finished sauce.

Roast the cumin seeds in a heavy pan. Add the garam masala, ground cumin, coriander, chilli powder and fresh chilli, fry gently.

Add to the spices the tomato puree and the salt. Bring to the boil, stirring all the time until the butter appears to separate out from the mixture. Reduce the heat and stir in the cream.

Taste and start adding a squeeze of lemon and a pinch of sugar and continue until the sauce is to your taste. Remove any skin and fat from the lamb and sear the meat in a heavy pan. Add the meat and any juices from the pan to the sauce.

Bring to the boil, reduce the heat and steam cook (using tea towel and lid) for about 20 minutes until the lamb is tender.

Turn onto a serving dish and sprinkle with fresh coriander. Serve with basmati rice cooked with whole spices, cloves, black and green cardamom pods plus cinnamon stick. Once cooked, stir in a few raisins, flaked, toasted almonds and pistachio nuts.

(This recipe was 2nd prize winner in the 1991 Egon Ronay Guide's British Lamb Competition.)

Frances Kennedy

Shenstone

Spiced Coconut Lamb

2 lb lean lamb, cubed

1 large onion, chopped

4 cloves of garlic, crushed

2 ozs concentrated butter or ghee

1 tbls grated fresh ginger

1 level tsp turmeric

2 level tsps ground cumin

1 level tsp chilli powder

8 whole green cardomum seeds

4 cloves

½ pint water

½ pint single cream

2 ozs creamed coconut

2 ozs sultanas

Melt the butter in a large frying pan with a lid, add the onion and fry until soft and golden. Add the garlic and then the ginger, turmeric, cumin and chilli powder. Crush the cardomum sufficiently to let the little black seeds inside escape and add the pods and seeds to the pan. Fry gently for one minute.

Add the lamb and stir so that each piece is covered with the spice mixture. Add the water and cream and half a teaspoon of salt (this helps to bring out the seasonings). Bring to a simmer, cover the pan and cook for about an hour. You can transfer it to a casserole in the oven if you prefer.

When the lamb is tender, stir in the creamed coconut. I use the block and cut it into small pieces. Add the sultanas and reheat gently. Garnish with chopped fresh coriander or toasted flaked almonds.

Although this dish has spices in it, it is aromatic, very pretty and you would be hard pressed to spot the garlic! Try it on a garlic/spice hater.

(This recipe came from Woman's Journal, a few years ago).

Frances Kennedy
Shenstone

Mushroom Stuffed Shoulder

3 lb shoulder lamb

1 oz butter

1 onion, finely chopped

2 oz ham, chopped

8 oz mushrooms, chopped

salt and pepper

2 tbls fresh mint, chopped

8 fl oz chicken stock

2 cloves garlic, halved

2 tbls oil

Plain flour to thicken

8 fl oz vegetable stock

Ask your butcher to bone the shoulder of lamb for you. The joint will be tied after being stuffed.

Heat oven to 180°C/325°F/gas mark 4. Melt butter in frying pan. Add ham, onions, mushrooms and fry for 3 minutes until onion is soft. Stir in seasonings and mint. Allow to cool.

Stuff the cavity of the meat. Tie with string at intervals. Place meat in roasting tin and chicken stock and garlic, brush with oil. Roast for 2 hours or until cooked.

Transfer meat to serving dish and allow meat to relax and therefore make it easier to carve. Make gravy using juices and little fat from tin. Thicken with flour and add vegetable stock.

Good served with roast potatoes and seasonal vegetables.

(Serves 6)

Bronwen Watts
Swansea

Lamb Goulash (Cooked in its Own Skin)

4 lbs lean lamb (cut into 1"-2" chunks, removing most of the visible fat)

2 lbs onion (peeled and roughly chopped)

4 tablespoons mild paprika powder (use more if your taste prefers)

2 fresh sweet red peppers (de-seeded and cut into chunks)

1 teaspoon caraway seeds

1 teaspoon salt

Half pint sour cream (optional)

2 tablespoons plain flour (optional)

Brown the lamb and onions together for a few minutes until onions are translucent. Add paprika and stir well. Add the caraway seeds, salt and peppers and stir well. Cover tightly and cook gently for half an hour over a low heat. Do *not* add any liquid.

Remove pan from heat and wrap in one or more sheepskin rugs (or sheepskin coats). Leave overnight.

Unwrap in the morning and allow to cool. When ready to eat, heat up very gently. The meat should be very tender. If a richer gravy is required, stir the flour into the soured cream until there are no lumps, then add gently to the warmed goulash. Bring just to boiling point and serve.

Serve with baked potatoes or 'penne' type pasta or more authentically, home made gnoche or noodles. On the side a cucumber salad.

William Macdonald
Gartocharn

Piquant Henry

4 oz raisins

4 oz dried apricots, halved

1 pt dry cider

2.5 lbs meat (boned shoulder, for example)

1 oz flour

quarter teaspoon ground cumin

quarter teaspoon paprika

2-3 tbls oil

1 large onion, chopped

4 oz button mushrooms, halved

1 green pepper, seeded and diced

Stock as required (about half a pint)

2 bay leaves

salt and pepper

What to do with a 5 year old Castlemilk Moorit ram put into the freezer in June. This is an excellent recipe for any sheep meat that needs long slow cooking.

Put raisins and apricots into a bowl with the cider, cover and leave overnight. Next day, cut the meat into two-inch chunks. Mix the flour, cumin and paprika together and toss the meat in the seasoned flour. Reserve any remaining flour.

Heat the oil in a casserole and brown the meat all over. Drain and remove the meat from the casserole. Gently fry all the vegetables in the oil until softened. Sprinkle the remaining flour over the vegetables, cook gently stirring until golden. Remove from the heat and gradually stir in the stock. Add the fruits and cider, the meat, bay leaves and seasoning to the casserole. Bring to the boil, stirring then reduce the heat. Put on lid and simmer gently.

Cooking time depends on age of animal and source of heat. Aga slow oven for a 5 year old ram is about 3-4 hours.

Di Roberts

Beef Recipes

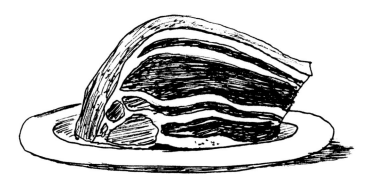

Oxtail Stew

1 ox tail

2 oz plain flour

2 oz dripping

2 small carrots

2 small onions

Salt and pepper

1 ½ pints beef stock or water

Wash tail well and dry it. Cut into joints and trim off any excess fat. Dip in flour. Melt fat in saucepan and fry meat till brown. Lift out meat and lightly fry sliced carrots and onions. Put meat back into the saucepan, add seasoning and stock or water. Simmer for 3 hours. Serves 4.

Nicky Guthrie
Inverness

Beef Olives

4 thin slices of beef topside*

1 large onion

6 hard-boiled egg yolks

1 tbls (15 ml) shredded suet

2 tsps (10 ml) finely chopped parsley

A pinch of ground ginger

A pinch of powdered saffron

Salt

A little butter

Cider vinegar for sprinkling

**A little ground ginger, cinnamon and
   black pepper, mixed, for sprinkling**

Olives

Beat the meat thin and flat with a cutlet bat. Chop the onion finely with 4 egg yolks. Add the suet, parsley, ginger, saffron and salt to taste. Knead and squeeze until pasty, using the onion liquid to bind. (If necessary, add a few drops of water or a little extra parsley.)

Spread the stuffing on the meat slices and roll them up like small Swiss rolls. Secure with wooden toothpicks. Lay side by side in a greased baking tin, with the cut edges underneath. Dot with butter. Bake, turning once, at gas mark 4/350°F/180°C for 35-40 minutes. Baste once or twice while baking.

Lay the olives on a warmed serving dish. Just before serving, sprinkle with vinegar and spices, and garnish with the remaining egg yolks, crumbled.

*Lamb rump can be used if preferred.

"A Taste of History"
English Heritage

Oxtail in Stout

1 ox tail (cut into pieces)

6ozs/175g chopped kidney

3 medium onions (finely sliced)

3-4 carrots (sliced)

1oz/25g flour

1 tsp brown sugar

Salt and pepper to taste

1 pint Stout

2/3 pickled walnuts

1 tbls of juice

Brown the sliced onions and carrots, add oxtail and brown. Sprinkle them with the flour, salt and pepper and brown sugar. Add kidney and stir in the stout. Tip all into a casserole. Cover and cook slowly till meat almost drops off bones. Leave to cool next day and remove fat. Reheat and add 2 or 3 pickled walnuts and 1 tablespoon of juice.

Ann How

Market Harborough

Beef Diane

4 x 6oz rump steaks, trimmed of fat

4oz unsalted butter

Juice and rind of half a lemon

1 tbls chopped parsley

1 clove of garlic

1 dsp caster sugar

Worcester sauce

Brandy for flaming - 3-4 tbls

Cut each steak in half. Beat them flat with a rolling pin, until less than ¼ in. thick. Place on a tray separated by cling film. Grate the lemon rind finely.

Melt 2oz butter in a large frying pan, crush the garlic into this. When the butter foams, fry the steaks quickly. About 30 seconds each side and keep warm.

Melt the other 2oz butter in pan, add the lemon juice and rind, the parsley, caster sugar and Worcester sauce to taste. Heat through, return the steaks to the pan and coat in the sauce.

Add the brandy and set alight. Serve with creamed potatoes and a suitable vegetable.

(Serves 4)

The Duchess of Wellington

Goulash

3 lbs braising steak trimmed and cubed

2 tbls paprika

1 tbls tomato purée

14 oz can tomatoes;

2 green peppers de-seeded and coarsely chopped

2 large onions coarsely chopped

½ lb mushrooms chopped

¾ pint meat stock

2 cloves garlic

Pinch caraway seeds

1 bay leaf

Salt and pepper

2 tbls olive oil

Heat oil in large heavy based frying pan. Fry onions and chopped garlic until soft but not brown. Add peppers and mushrooms, fry until soft and add paprika, chopped tomatoes, caraway seeds and bay leaf.

Remove from pan and place in casserole dish. Add meat to frying pan and brown on all sides. Add to onion mixture and add stock. Season to taste.

Heat oven to 170°C/325°F/gas mark 3. Cover and cook for 2-2½ hrs. Serve with baked potatoes and sour cream.

Bronwen Watts
Swansea

Cawl *(Welsh Broth)*

2 lbs lean brisket (on the bone) or shin beef

1 large onion, chopped

2 carrots, cubed

2 small parsnips, cubed

¼ small swede, cubed

4 potatoes, peeled and halved

1 lb leeks washed and coarsely chopped

Parsley, chopped

Salt and pepper

2 tsps plain flour, mixed with water for thickening

Place meat in large saucepan with 3 pints water. Bring to boil and skim off any scum that may appear. Add seasoning and simmer until meat is almost tender. Add vegetables and cook for further 20-30 minutes.

Add leeks and parsley and thickening, cook for further 5 minutes.

This is a traditional Carmarthen recipe. Other regions of Wales use lamb or mutton in place of beef.

Bronwen Watts
Swansea

Chilli con Carne

1 tbls oil

1 oz butter

2 finely chopped medium onions

2 cloves crushed garlic

4 oz chopped trimmed bacon

1½ lbs minced beef

2½ oz puréed tomatoes

¾ pt water

½-1 tsp fresh chilli powder

16 oz canned red kidney beans

Heat oil and butter in large heavy saucepan. Fry onions and garlic until brown. Remove from saucepan. Add bacon and mince to pan. Fry until brown, return onions to pan. Add all other ingredients. Cover, turn heat down and simmer very gently for 2½ hrs.

Empty kidney beans into fresh saucepan and bring to boil quickly stirring gently to prevent beans sticking to base. As soon as they have boiled, remove from heat, tip into colander and wash in warm water. Add to meat mixture ½ hr before end of cooking time.

Bronwen Watts

Swansea

Ox Tongue with Mushrooms

Tongue:

1 small ox tongue (or 8-10 lambs tongues)

1 large onion

1 bay leaf

2 outside stalks of celery

A little salt

4 peppercorns

Cold water

Sauce:

1 oz butter

1 fl oz oil

1 oz flour

1 level dsp French mustard

8-12 oz mushrooms

2-4 small finely chopped pickled gherkins

½ pt cider

5 fl oz thick double cream (optional)

If tongue is salted, soak overnight in cold water (change water after 3-4 hrs if poss.). Change to fresh water and bring to boil, add halved onion, bay leaf, celery, salt and peppercorns. Simmer very gently in covered pan allowing 40 mins. per lb. Meanwhile, heat butter and oil in pan, de-stalk mushrooms (and halve if large; break up if horse-mushrooms and chop up stalk) and fry briskly.

Remove mushrooms and stalks and return all butter/oil to pan. Fry gherkins and slowly work in flour. Gradually thin down with cider. Stir in French mustard and mushrooms and stalks. Boil down tongue stock and add up to 1 pt to mushroom sauce. Remove skin of tongue and any tiny bones at root end. Slice thickly or dice and place into casserole with lid and cover with sauce.

Cook at 125°C/250°F/gas mark 1 for 1hr 30min - till piping hot.

Stir in cream before serving.

Mrs Jennie Harvey-Hull
Dorset

Boerewors (Farmers' Sausage)

3 lb minced pork

3 lb minced beef

2 tsps salt

1 tsp pepper

½ tsp grated nutmeg

2 dsps. whole coriander

½ tsp ground cloves

½ tsp cup vinegar

Combine all ingredients thoroughly, and put into well rinsed, natural sausage skins. Can be frozen - defrost thoroughly before cooking. Best cooked on a braai, or grilled.

(This has been taken from a book put together by the women of the Valley Methodist Church - SOMEWHERE in South Africa.)

Kathy Smith
Banbury

Dexter Beefsteak Pie

1 lb stewing steak

Beef dripping or oil olive

1 large onion skinned and sliced

2 level tbls flour

Beef stock

1 stick celery, chopped

1 carrot, chopped

1 leek, chopped

½ lb tomatoes, chopped

Thyme, oregano and parsley

Bay leaf

Salt and pepper

Shortcrust pastry

Red wine (optional)

Cut the meat into 1 inch cubes and fry a few cubes at a time in the hot dripping or olive oil until brown on all sides. Remove with a slotted spoon. Fry the onions, the carrot, celery and leek in the pan to soak up all the residue from the meat. Add the chopped tomatoes and herbs and season to taste, cook for a few more minutes.

Place the vegetables and meat in a casserole. Pour the red wine into the pan and reduce till almost dry. Add some of the stock, stir round to collect all the bits from the frying, then pour into the casserole, cover with the remaining stock and season to taste. Bring to the boil then put the lid on and transfer to a pre-heated oven 170°C/325°F/gas mark 3 for 2 hours.

Remove the pieces of meat and the bay leaf from the casserole and keep on one side. Press the remaining veg. and sauce through a sieve, or put in a blender.

Place the meat in a pie dish and cover with the sauce. Leave to cool.

Roll out the pastry and cover the pie dish, dampening the edges, trim and flake the edges. Decorate if you wish and brush with beaten egg. Bake in the oven at 220°C/425°F/gas mark 7 for 20 minutes then reduce to 180°C/350°F/gas mark 4 for about a further ¼ hour.

Mrs Robert Geering
Woodchurch

Potted Brisket of Dexter Beef

1 boned & rolled joint of Brisket

1 onion (sliced)

1 carrot (sliced)

1 stick celery (sliced)

1 small swede (chopped)

1 leek (sliced)

Beef dripping

Salt & pepper

Mace blades

Melted butter

Beef stock

Sear the joint in the hot dripping until brown on all sides and remove from pan. Brown all the vegetables in the pan, then replace the beef and add the stock, enough to cover the vegetables and come halfway up the beef. Add salt and pepper and a couple of mace blades. Bring to the boil then cover and place in oven 170°C/325°F/gas mark 3 for about 3 hours. When cooked remove from oven and allow to cool. Remove joint from casserole and take off strings. Trim fat off meat and discard. Chop meat into small bits and mix in some of the melted butter. Pack into a basin or mould and pour enough melted butter on to almost cover meat. Chill in fridge until butter is set.

Serve with salad or can be spread in sandwiches, depending on how small the meat is chopped.

The vegetable stock can be made into a delicious soup.

Mrs Robert Geering
Woodchurch

Poultry Recipes

Roast Turkey the Genteel Way
(Hannah Glasse, 1747)

1 Bronze Turkey

For the forcemeat:

A large fowl or 1lb/500g of veal

Same quantity of grated bread

8oz/240g suet

A little mace

2 cloves

Half grated nutmeg

1 tbls grated lemon peel

2 eggs (yolks only)

Salt & pepper to taste

First cut turkey down the back, and with a sharp penknife bone it, then make your force-meat thus: take a large fowl, or a pound of veal, as much grated bread, half a pound of suet cut and beat very fine, a little beaten mace, two cloves, half a nutmeg grated, about a large teaspoonful of lemon peel, and the yolks of two eggs; mix all together, with a little pepper and salt, fill up the places where the bones came out, and fill the body, that it may look just as it did before, sew up the back, and roast it. You may have oyster sauce, celery sauce, or just as you please; but good gravy in the dish, and garnish with lemon, is as good as anything. Be sure to leave the pinions on.

Anne Wilson
Doncaster

Escalloped Chicken

6 lb/3kg hen

1 cup chicken fat

1 cup flour

Salt & pepper to taste

4 cups broth

2 cups milk

4 cups corn bread crumbs

1 cup finely chopped celery

One-third cup finely chopped onion

1 teaspoon salt

Black pepper

One-third cup melted butter

Cook a 6 pound hen until tender. Remove from broth, cool, remove meat from bones. Cut into large bite sized pieces, set aside. Melt the chicken fat and blend with the flour. Season with 1 teaspoon salt and black pepper to taste. Slowly add broth and milk - stir constantly. Cook over medium heat until sauce thickens.

Dressing mixture: Combine the corn bread crumbs with the finely chopped celery and onion, salt and black pepper to taste and melted butter.

Arrange the chicken and dressing mixture in alternate layers in a very large casserole dish. Cover with sauce and bake 1 hour at 350°F/180°C/gas mark 4. Makes 16 servings.

Jan Palmer
Oklahoma, USA

Chicken Casserole

2 cups each cooked chicken (cubed)

Milk

Raw macaroni

2 cans cream of chicken soup

Cheese slices

Mix all together and put in a baking dish. Refrigerate overnight. Just before baking, cover with cheese slices. Bake at 325°F/170°C/gas mark 3 for 1 hour.

Jan Palmer
Oklahoma, USA

Chicken Pie Supreme

Pastry for 2 crust pie

1 whole stewing chicken (5 pound)

3 pts/1½ quarts water

2 tsps salt

1 small onion

1 carrot

1 branch celery

½ cup sifted flour

½ tsp onion salt and celery salt (or use onion powder if reducing salt)

dash of pepper

3½ cups chicken broth

Can be made ahead and frozen for busy days.

Place chicken in large pan with water, 1 teaspoon salt, onion, carrot and celery. Simmer, covered, until tender, 3-3½ hours. Remove chicken and strip meat from bones in large pieces. Refrigerate chicken and broth to cool.

Combine flour, onion salt (or powder), celery salt, pepper and 1 teaspoon salt with ½ cup cooled chicken broth. Mix until smooth. Put 3 cups chicken broth in skillet; heat and add flour mixture, beating with a wire whip to prevent lumping.

Cook over medium heat, stirring constantly, until mixture is smooth and thickened. Add chicken and blend well. Cool. Line a 9 inch deep dish pie pan with pastry. Fill with cooled chicken mixture. Adjust top crust; cut vents and seal edges. Makes 6-8 servings. Freeze pie. When frozen, wrap securely, label, date and return to freezer. Stores 3-6 months. Cool remaining broth and freeze in glass jars or freezer containers.

To serve, bake frozen pie in hot oven 400°F/200°C/gas mark 6 for 45 minutes to 1 hour. Chicken filling should be hot, the crust a golden brown. Make gravy with frozen broth to serve with pie.

Jan Palmer
Oklahoma, USA

Dorking Cottagers' Pie

3 lb Dorking chicken including liver

1 lb lean Tamworth pork

1 lb Tamworth belly pork

4 rashers Tamworth bacon

1 shallot

¾ lb puff pastry

1 beaten Maran egg

Remove chicken skin. Cut breast in long thin slices. Mince pork, belly pork and rest of chicken meat and liver. Mix with a little salt and pepper. Chop shallot finely and mix in. Line casserole with two-thirds of the puff pastry. Lay 2 bacon rashers on the bottom. Fill with alternate layers of mince and breast. Cover last layer of mince with rest of bacon and cover with remaining pastry. Keep a little pastry for decoration, if required. Make a hole for the steam. Brush with beaten egg. Bake at 450°F/230°C/gas mark 8 for 30 mins, then turn down to 350°F/180°C/gas mark 4, cover top with wet greaseproof paper and cook for a further 1 hour.

Timothy & Anne Wilson
Doncaster

Giblets á la Bagration

Giblets, livers, neck and feet from turkey, chicken or goose

Salt

Cold water

6 pints (approx) stock

3-4 onions (chopped)

2 leeks (sliced)

6 peppercorns

Coralline pepper

Blade of mace

4 cloves

Good bunch herbs (thyme/parsley/bayleaf/basil/marjoram)

Arrowroot or glass of sherry

Boiled macaroni

Fresh parsley

Take the giblets from turkey, chicken or goose, cut the livers in four or five pieces, clean the gizzards and cut in six or eight pieces, cut the neck in lengths of about 1½ inches, skin the feet, and put all into a saucepan, with a little salt and enough water to cover it; let it come to the boil, then strain off and wash the pieces in cold water. Put them into sufficient stock to cover them well; add vegetables, peppercorns, a good dust of coralline pepper, mace, cloves and herbs. Bring gently to the boil, skim well, and let it simmer for about 3 hours. Strain off, take out the meat from the vegetables and set it aside to serve in the soup, let the stock stand to cool, then remove any fat from it, and clarify; strain it through a clean cloth, put it back into a clean pan, and for each 2 pints mix a dessertspoonful of the best arrowroot with a little of the stock or a glass of sherry; stir it into the soup till it thickens, and then add the pieces of meat, taking care that they are well rinsed with a little warm water before adding to the soup. To each 2 pints of the soup add a tablespoonful of boiled macaroni, and serve leaves of parsley picked and blanched, in the soup.

(From "Mrs A B Marshall's Cookery Book" Published 1885).

Nicky Guthrie

Inverness

Capon with Orange or Lemon Sauce

1 capon or chicken

1 pint (575 ml) chicken stock

2 oz (50g) currants

4 dates

about 8 oz (225g) oranges, mandarins or lemons

½ tsp (2.5 ml) black peppercorns

1 tsp (5 ml) blade mace

3 tbls (45 ml) sugar

1 tbls (15 ml) rosewater

¼ pint (150 ml) white wine or claret

8 oz (225g) white bread, cut into large crustless cubes

Put the capon or chicken in a pan, cover with water and boil until tender, 45 minutes being sufficient for a tender bird, although 3-4 hours may be required for a genuine boiling fowl. Drain 1 pint (575 ml) stock from bird, and simmer for 5 minutes with the currants, dates, and fruit, peeled and divided into individual segments. Then add the remaining ingredients (white wine being preferable when using lemons), simmer for a further 5-10 minutes, and pour over the bird arranged on a bed of bread cubes in a large dish.

"A Taste of History"
English Heritage

Guinea Fowl in Cream

1 Guinea Fowl

8 small onions

1½ ozs butter

½ pt double cream

1 tbls lemon juice

1 tbls redcurrant jelly

Blanch onions and fry together with fowl in butter until browned. Add cream, salt and pepper. Cover and cook slowly for 2-3 hours, remove fowl, add lemon juice and redcurrant jelly to make a sauce.

Ann How
Market Harborough

Chicken with Tarragon

For each bird you will need:

1 tablespoon of chopped tarragon

1 clove of garlic

2oz/50g butter

A little brandy

Double cream

A little Madeira

Salt & pepper to taste

Work the tarragon and garlic into the butter and stuff mixture into each bird. Cover birds with olive oil and roast until cooked. Flambé with brandy and leave to mature in a low oven for 10 minutes. Remove birds from pan and make a sauce in the pan with the double cream, madeira and salt and pepper to taste.

Ann How
Market Harborough

Festive Chicken

2 Chicken breasts, boned and skinned

1 oz cooked, peeled prawns

1 oz Gruyere cheese, cut into very small dice

1 oz wholemeal flour

1 oz butter

¼ pt creme fraiche

3 tablespoons brandy

Salt and pepper

½ teaspoon french mustard

Slice each chicken breast through the thickest part but do not cut it right through. Open each one out, cover with cling film and beat with a rolling pin to spread out.

Chop the prawns roughly and put half the prawns and half the diced cheese into each breast. Fold over carefully to enclose the filling and press down well, especially around the edges.

Dip into the flour and fry in hot butter for 6-7 minutes each side. Remove the chicken from the pan and put onto a serving dish to keep warm while you make the sauce. Pour the brandy into the pen and set alight. As soon as the flames have died down add the creme fraiche, salt and pepper and the mustard. Reduce slightly, check the seasoning and pour over the chicken.

Serve immediately. Don't keep it standing about because of the prawns.

Frances Kennedy
Shenstone

Flaming Chicken Livers

227g Chicken livers

4 medium button mushrooms

25g butter

1 tbs olive oil

1 small onion

1 clove garlic

2 tbls brandy

200g creme fraiche

Salt and pepper

8 1" slices cut at the diagonal from a French stick

4 tbs. olive oil

100g Red Pesto

1 tbls chopped coriander leaves

1 bag washed, assorted salad leaves

Peel and chop onion finely. Peel and crush garlic. Drain and cut livers into small pieces. Wipe and slice mushrooms. Slice bread. Mix the 4 tbls olive oil into the pesto and dip both sides of the bread slices into it. Place on grill rack. Chop coriander and put salad into serving bowl.

Light grill. Heat 25g butter and 1 tbls oil in a shallow, enamelled, cast iron dish which can be taken from cooker to table. Quickly fry the onion and garlic for 1 min. Put bread under grill and toast both sides. Add livers to pan with the onion and garlic mixture and toss over a high flame for 1 min. Add brandy to pan and set alight. As soon as flames die down, add creme fraiche to pan. Bring to boil, check seasoning and remove from heat. Place the toasted bread in a circle around the edge of the dish, sprinkle the liver mixture with the chopped coriander. Serve with a green salad. Eat and enjoy!

(Serves 2)

Frances Kennedy
Shenstone

Easter Chicken

Chicken joints

½ tsp salt

1 level tbls Demerara sugar

½ tsp Ground Ginger

3 oranges

1 dsp Paprika

½ pt giblet stock

1 level tbls flour

1 oz butter

Season the chicken with the salt and paprika. Fry in the butter until golden. Remove the chicken from the pan and add the flour, salt and ginger. Stir well and gather up all the juices from the base of the pan.

Add the juice of 3 oranges and the zest of 2. Stir over a gentle heat until the mixture thickens. Add the chicken and simmer until cooked.

Frances Kennedy
Shenstone

Spicy Chicken Starters

2½ lb chicken wings

3 tbls soy sauce

3 tbls light brown sugar

2 tbls corn oil

1 tsp dry mustard

2 tbls dry sherry

6 tbls tomato ketchup

Arrange chicken wings in single layer in dish. Mix together soy sauce, sugar, oil, mustard and sherry in a saucepan. Heat gently until sugar dissolves. Pour over chicken wings and leave to marinate, for minimum of 1 hour*. Heat oven to 180°C/350°F/gas mark 4. Cook chicken wings in marinade for 50-60 minutes basting occasionally.

Arrange chicken wings in serving dish. Drain fat from cooking dish. Mix tomato ketchup with 4 tablespoons of remaining marinade. Pour into a small bowl. Sprinkle chicken wings with chopped parsley.

These are excellent 'finger' food as an appetiser or lunchbox or picnic treat. They can be served as a main meal dish.

*Tip - Chicken wings may be left to marinate for longer (or overnight) but use a glass dish.

(Serves 4)

Bronwen Watts
Swansea

Orange Roast Chicken

3½ lb fresh chicken

1 oz butter

1 small onion, finely chopped

2 large cloves garlic, finely chopped

2 ozs celery, finely chopped

5 oz fresh breadcrumbs

½ tsp dried rosemary

2 tbls chopped fresh parsley

Salt and pepper to taste

2 oranges

2 tbls olive oil

2 fl oz white wine

Fresh watercress and orange twists to garnish

½ pint hot chicken stock

Melt butter in pan and sauté onions, garlic and celery until soft. Add breadcrumbs, half the rosemary and parsley. Grate rind from one orange and add to stuffing mixture. Peel oranges and chopped flesh, add to stuffing mixture.

The stuffing is much improved by preparing it 24 hrs ahead, covering with cling film and storing in refrigerator. Spoon stuffing into chicken, brush with oil and sprinkle with remaining rosemary. Roast in a pre-heated oven 190°C/375°F/gas mark 5 for 1½-2 hrs, basting with juices and wine.

Transfer chicken to serving dish and garnish with watercress and orange twists. Skim fat from juices in roasting tin, add chicken stock and heat through to make gravy. Good served with roast potatoes and parsnips and lightly steamed carrots.

Bronwen Watts

Swansea

SOURCES OF SUPPLY OF RARE BREED MEAT

Mr G Loder
Loders (Yeovil) Ltd
Union Street
Yeovil
Somerset
BA20 1PQ
Tel: 01935 21503

Mr J Brown
J Brown Butchers
73 Rances Lane
Wokingham
Berkshire
RG11 2LG
Tel: 01734 786258

S J Harvell, Butchers
The Butchers Shop
The Chalk
Iwerne Minster
Blandford
Dorset
DT11 8NA
Tel: 01747 811229

Mr P Graves
H V Graves, Butchers
24 Gladstone Place
Briston
Melton Constable
Norfolk
NR24 2LE
Tel: 01263 860333

David Lishman, Butchers
25 Leeds Road
Ilkley
Leeds
Yorkshire
LS29 8DP
Tel: 01943 609436

F C Phipps, Butchers
Osborne House
Mareham le Fen
Boston
Lincolnshire
PE22 7RW
Tel: 01507 568235

Mr & Mrs K Smith
Sladden Farm
Alkham Valley
Nr. Dover
Kent CT15 7BX
Tel: 01304 825188

Mrs H Ellis
Bursea Farm Shop
Holme on Spalding Moor
York YO4 7DB
Tel: 01430 860348

Mrs C M Mack
Norwood Farm
Bath Road
Norton St Philip
Bath BA3 6LP
Tel: 01373 834356

Mr N Charrington
Layer Marney Tower
Colchester
Essex CO5 9US
Tel: 01206 330784

Gary Wallace
Chesterton Farm Butchery
Chesterton Lane
Cirencester
Gloucestershire
GL7 6JP
Tel: 01285 642160

Mrs Anne Petch
Heal Farm
Quality Traditional Meats
Kings Nympton
Umberleigh
Devon EX37 9TB
Tel: 01769 574341
(Mail orders available)

Mr R H L Lutwyche
The Cotswold Gourmet
PO Box 26
Cirencester
Gloucestershire
GL7 5TJ
Tel: 01285 860229